I0470971

# How Bright is My Future?

## Dare to Step into Your Vision

Jean Shaffer

ISBN-13: 978-1484085714
ISBN-10: 148408571X

# DEDICATION

This book is dedicated to my late father, James Maxwell Vickers, who purchased and learned to use a computer when he was in his 80's and wrote his World War II memoirs.  In doing so, he left a great legacy for his children, grandchildren, great-grandchildren, and those to come.  And to my mother, Doris Barnes Vickers, who slept on the sofa for over a year so that I could start my next chapter.

# ACKNOWLEDGMENTS

Janice Vickers – Copy Editor
Luca Rugiero – cover photo Sunglasses at the Beach.
Joseph Campbell quotations:
The Joseph Campbell Foundation
Apostrophe S Productions:
Joseph Campbell and The Power of Myth with Bill Moyers

# TABLE OF CONTENTS

# INTRODUCTION

My hope is that this book will be the first step in creating an exciting  vision for your future; at the very least, reduce anxiety about potential change.

My youngest grandchild just graduated from her crib to a "big girl bed," and I wanted to cry.  Why are we always surprised at how quickly time flies?  I get sick of hearing myself say it.  Every year I do my taxes on Super Bowl Sunday, and every year I'm surprised that it's "that" time again.

Recently, I conducted a survey asking people to select a word that best describes their feelings about the future.  The options were Excited, OK, Concerned, Anxious, Terrified.  The participants age 55 and older responded with the latter 3.

According to AARP, 44 % of retirees work for pay at some point after retirement, due to either monetary needs or other reasons.  Furthermore, only 36 % of Americans ages 40 – 58 and 47 % age 59–70, are confident they will have enough money to live comfortably in retirement.

There are many resources for people wanting to explore retirement options or to live a fulfilling retirement. This book is for people who either want or need to continue in their current careers, or want to explore options to generate additional income to supplement their retirement incomes.

What we can accomplish in one year is amazing. One year consists of a string of hours that are flying by and yet hold the secret to our happiness. Most of us are not fully aware of the power we possess to create the future that we want and deserve.

You can read this book easily in one sitting, but I hope you will take the survey first, then read one chapter at a time. There are thirteen chapters that are quick and easy to read, and each chapter ends with one small action step. I also encourage you to write something or someone you are grateful for.

By the end of the book, you will have thirteen small action steps that can change your life by stepping into your vision.

I hope you will:
- *Feel empowered and encouraged to create the future you want.*

2

- *Be inspired to change the way you think about age.*
- *Commit to specific action steps to move forward **now**.*
- *Accept possibility and prepare for unplanned future challenges.*
- *Identify resources needed for planning.*

I look forward to hearing from you as we take a look at the future …

# THE SURVEY

Many people have pondered, "How did we get from 2000 to today so quickly?" Have you considered how old will you be in the year 2030? Ouch. Millions of Baby Boomers, now in their late 50's, are wondering how they can survive in the workplace one more decade (or more), and after that, will they have the financial resources to survive what could be a substantial number of retirement years. Not to worry, 68 is fast becoming the new 58. Honest.

Let's not kid ourselves, the next decade will fly by at the speed of light. So, do you have a plan to take you from today to the future? Do you plan to just coast or float into the next decade, and then deal with what you find there? Have you reflected on the events of the last decade? What lessons did you learn? Were you happy? Why or why not? Were some of the worst years also your best years? What might be different now, if you had developed a ten-year plan?

Following are some questions to help you assess if you are prepared to *thrive* in your latter stages of work:

1. I believe my employer will be loyal to me as long as I work really hard to meet and exceed their expectations. Agree/Disagree.

2.  I make every effort to go above and beyond expectations in my current position.  Agree/Disagree.
3.  I live a healthy lifestyle which includes building fun (non work) activities into my weekly schedule. Agree/Disagree.
4.  I am terrified when I think about my financial future. Agree/Disagree.
5.  I am tired of working so hard and feel angry when I think about how my current or former employers have disappointed me.  Agree/Disagree.
6.  Each year I assess my talents and reflect on what I enjoy, and seek out projects that energize me. Agree/Disagree.
7.  Each year I review and develop career management/ professional development goals that include networking with other professionals and joining professional organizations. Agree/Disagree.
8.  Each year I update my Brand or my Resume and spend some time researching industry trends and exploring new and challenging opportunities. Agree/Disagree.
9.  I have a transition plan that I can quickly implement if I lose my current position. Agree/Disagree.
10. I sometimes dwell on decisions or choices I made in the past that have had a negative financial impact on me or my family.  Agree/Disagree.
11. I stay abreast of trends in my industry and profession. Agree/Disagree.
12. I am aware of opportunities with my current employer and also the challenges and priorities they face in advancing the business. Agree/Disagree.

# MY STORY

Like it or not, I'll be 68 in the year 2020, 78 in the year 2030, 88 in 2040, and 98 in 2050. My mother is 93.

I am proud of my accomplishments. I have helped tens of thousands of professionals during their career transitions, and it has been personally rewarding.

For much of my life I thought about retirement at age 66, a time when I would no longer work, and just do what I wanted to do—enjoy hobbies, travel, hang out with friends and family.

However, like many people, I had to realize that retirement is probably not going to happen as I had envisioned it for a number of reasons.

The combination of divorce, two job losses, and the recession created some financial challenges. I came to realize that the subconscious vision I had for the future would not be realized.

In the 90's, I was burned out on my corporate job and my daily commute in Atlanta. It took a demotion, disguised as a lateral move, to catalyze consideration for change.

Following my divorce, I decided to relocate to the coast and applied for a position.  While I was waiting to receive an offer, I purchased a print of tropical fish and announced to my friends that I would hang the print in my new home when I landed this position.  I did accept the offer and the print still hangs in my hallway.  It's a daily reminder of the power of vision.

Later, it was a downsizing that forced me out of my comfort zone, and I finally recognized that it is up to me to create a new vision of my future that makes me feel optimistic about the future instead of anxious.  Life is too short to pursue work that you don't really want.  Sometimes, it takes a major upheaval to spur us into change.  For me, the divorce motivated me to finish my degree.

I have been successful at reinventing myself, progressing from Pediatric Assistant, Secretary, Retail Trainer, Corporate Trainer, Training & Development Manager, Independent Consultant, Instructional Designer, to Career Consultant and author.

As a Career Coach, I've worked with thousands of clients in their 50's who were downsized and anxious about the future.  I have friends who are concerned, even terrified about having adequate financial resources.

The financial media has done a thorough job of scaring the Baby Boomers to death. OK, we get it. Let's look at solutions.

I choose to not spend the last third of my life worried; rather confident that I can be creative and resourceful. I will also be happier if I continue to learn and enjoy intellectual challenges. I am now focused on getting excited about the next 30+ years of my life – my next and best chapters of my life. I invite you to join me.

# Chapter 1
*After all I've done for you.*

I believe my employer will be loyal to me as long as I work really hard to meet and exceed their expectations

If you answered *Agree* – be careful. Many loyal employees have been shocked to learn that their positions were eliminated.  It is naïve to assume that employers care about you and value your loyalty.  They value what you can do for them now.  Senior Managers are often too concerned about their own careers and retirement to worry about staff needs.  Focus on ways to make them look good while working on your influencing, persuasion, selling, and negotiation skills, which includes finessing the art of the "push back."  We can also appreciate the stability and benefits while they last.

If you approach every opportunity with the priority of doing your best and gaining new skills and expertise, you will be able to secure great references from managers, peers, and customers when you leave the position.

Some of you may stay with your current employer until retirement, and happily so. Some of you could be caught off guard, and lose your job due to a reorganization a few years earlier than you would like. Some of my clients have confided in me that they had become complacent in their careers.

It's important that employees understand the priorities of management and attempt to exceed expectations. There are some other strategies to be seen as an asset to the organization. First, having unique expertise or being seen as a Subject Matter Expert (SME) is a way to set you apart from the crowd.

Relationships with your peers across the organization, your superiors, and other senior managers require time and effort to develop. Are you well-known throughout the organization? Are you seen as someone who offers solutions to corporate challenges or team challenges? Even with mastery in all of these areas, there are no guarantees, right or wrong.

We have to let go of our old paradigms around loyalty, and think in a more entrepreneurial vein. It would be great, if we could do this without feeling stressed. Designing a future that you want is the best way to let go of the past. Empowering yourself to pursue what you want in life allows you to release a paralyzing victim mentality.

Consider your brand. I use the buzz-word "brand" reluctantly, but it is useful in considering these questions more honestly. How well are you known in the organization? In your profession? In your industry? What do people know about you? Whether we like it or not, the way we look is part of our brand, including our hairstyle, glasses, and wardrobe.

Volunteer or seek out opportunities/projects to work with associates from across the organization and stay in touch.

Social Media provides a new forum for developing and promoting your brand, while developing relationships, and sharing helpful information.

While working in an internal consulting role, I recognized that clients were frequently expressing needs, concerns, and problems that I might overlook. I learned to ask probing questions, actively listen, and say "I could help you with that," even if I wasn't sure how I might help. It frequently led to high visibility projects.

**Ray of Light –** *Ed was a successful sales representative for over 17 years before losing his job in a reorganization. He had contributed millions in sales to the organization. He was in his 40's and decided that he no longer wanted to be employed in corporate America. He invested in a well-established, family-owned business on the coast. The owner had just died, and the wife was selling the business, which was a good fit for Ed's skills and background. Ed started a new chapter. He has been very successful, even during the recession. When asked if he had any regrets, he says, "no, it was the best decision I ever made."*

**One small step –**

**Today, I am grateful for –**

# Chapter 2
*I've worked so hard.*

I make every effort to go above and beyond expectations in my current position.

If you answered *Disagree,* you might be at risk. Make every effort to go above and beyond expectations. However, keep in mind that it's up to you to maintain balance in your life. Remember the saying, "No one ever says, 'I wish I had spent more time at the office' on his/her death bed."

We need to realize and accept that strong performance is certainly important, but it in no way guarantees job security.

However, with that said, it's a good idea to review your most recent performance objectively and ask yourself if it was above expectations.

What you did two years ago or even last year is ancient history in today's environment of rapid change.

All of us, especially perfectionists and workaholics, should be mindful of the toll this stress could be taking on our health.

It's a lot to manage, but no one is going to do it for us.

Many of us at mid-life (40's to 60's) are wanting more balance in our lives. We are considering looking for more meaningful or satisfying work, taking a step down in responsibility, pursuing part-time work or starting a business.

At this stage, you may have put the kids through college and reduced your debt. By creating a five - ten year plan you can forecast your income and expenses. This can help you to be more proactive in getting the training, certification, or education you need to make a career change. Saving for a business and working on your business plan can be done while in your current career.

Sometimes when we feel stressed or dissatisfied, we simply need a vacation, or an attitude adjustment, and that should be a priority. Other times, we are in the right profession, but need a change or new environment to flourish.

Before you abandon your current career path, make sure you assess other areas of your life for sources of stress and frustration.

Ray of Light – *Approaching age 40, Bob had worked in telecommunications for almost 20 years, had been a recognized leader and survived numerous reorganizations. After becoming disillusioned, he decided to pursue a small consulting firm that recruited telecommunications professionals for contract assignments. He was also successful in this role. At age 50, he decided to start his own landscaping and lawn maintenance business in a high-end resort, where he lives. Once again, he transferred his management skills to a new role, and has been incredibly successful. This was not what he had envisioned in the 1970's, but he has been willing to reinvent himself, and is still not ready to retire.*

**One Small Step –**

**Today, I am grateful for –**

# *Chapter 3*
## *I work all the time.*

I live a healthy lifestyle which includes building fun (non-work) activities into my weekly schedule.

If you answered *Disagree*, "it's time to take care of your health so that you can really enjoy the last few decades, because they will require a lot of energy and ***resilience***. Do fun stuff.  Seriously.

Pay attention to your internal dialogue. What messages are you sending to your mind, body and spirit that could be depleting your energy?  How can you reframe those messages?

We spend a huge portion of our lives at work. What has been the personal cost of your hard work?  Do you feel like you are constantly swimming against the current? Hoping for that title, promotion, bonus, or recognition? How could things be different if we tried to swim ***with*** the current?  Maybe you haven't been drawing on your true talents and passions.

I realized that my vision of the future has involved having my grandchildren stay with me for a couple of weeks in the summer, like my children did with their grandparents who were retired.

So, I need to figure out how I can make that vision happen, and I will, but meanwhile I want to focus more on having fun now.

At least once a year, I like to ask myself these questions:

Am I growing?
Am I learning?
Am I loving?
Am I giving?
Am I having fun?

Thriving in this rapidly changing world requires resilience. Resilience is typically defined as the ability to recover quickly or bounce back from adversity. Another way to look at resilience is the ability to see opportunity in adversity.

Bouncing back is easier said than done. So what is an appropriate time frame to bounce back? 2 years? 2 months? 2 weeks? 2 days? 2 Hours? 2 minutes?

Most of us have had to deal with some type of disappointment or hurt in our lives, or we regret some action we did or did not take or choice that we made.

In the field of Training & Development, we must consider knowledge, skills, and attitudes in every learning objective.  All of these have relevance whether we are talking about careers or finance.

It's important to ask yourself if your view of the past could be preventing you from seeing the future in a new light or from recognizing opportunities in the present moment.

Reframing our attitude about the future starts with having an open mind that allows us to consider and create a new vision for the future.  How would you love to spend your time?

Does your vision include images of illness or living an active and physically fit lifestyle?  Need a little inspiration?  Check out the stories on AARP's "Life Reimagined."  The PBS documentary, Age of Champions, tells the story of five competitors ages 86 – 100 who swim, leap, and sprint for gold at the Senior Games.

**Ray of Light** – *Two years ago I was offered the opportunity to work on a project with a career guru, whom I idolize. I had already committed to a girls' weekend with two of my friends from childhood. Like many working moms, work, family, and chores usually won out over time with friends. I turned down the project and enjoyed the trip with my friends. We never know if our friends will be around or available for "next time." Having relationships outside of our families is one of the factors in having a balanced and fulfilling life.*

**One Small Step –**

**Today, I am grateful for –**

# Chapter 4

*I'll never be able to retire.*

I am terrified when I think about my financial future.

*The very cave you are afraid to enter turns out to be the source of what you are looking for.*

**- Joseph Campbell**

If you answered *Agree*, it would be helpful to address and test the rationale of your fears. Listen to your internal dialogue. What are you saying to yourself about the future? Do you think you would be happier if you had multi-millions in the bank? W...e...l...l – maybe for a little while. Then you might stress over losing it. It's amazing what you can accomplish in the next ten years.

When you consider your financial future, are you confident, ok, anxious, or terrified? What are your thoughts as you consider your response? Do you believe that you can change your thoughts about your financial future?

Wouldn't it be great if you met with a professional and learned that your financial future is better than you thought? If there is a gap in your monthly income and expenses, how much is it? Wouldn't it be best to know, so you can plan for that? You've probably already begun to reduce your debt and your expenses. At what point would you be able to downsize? Could you save an extra $100 per month?

Could you start taking courses now that would add credentials or certifications to your résumé?

Would a master's degree allow you to pursue an adjunct instructor position at a community college? Would the potential earnings offset the educational expense, or is there funding available?

Most financial institutions and investment firms have online retirement calculators to help you plan for retirement. These calculators will help you take a preliminary look at your situation. Your financial planner will require that you provide detailed information about your income, debt, savings, and expenses.

We have certainly had to deal with disappointments with our investments, real estate values, and job losses. It's helpful to reflect on our past in terms of lessons learned.

The Financial Action Plan chart on the right can give you a simplified high level snapshot to help you begin to plan for your encore career, which might require additional training or education.

If you want to start a business, you can plan ahead for the savings you will need and allow adequate time to develop an effective business plan.

A fee-based Certified Financial Planner will analyze and bring clarity to your financial needs, and provide multiple scenarios to consider. By using a fee-based Certified Financial Planner, you can avoid concerns about investment recommendations that may not be in your best interest.

The National Association of Personal Financial Advisors (www.napfa.org) offers The *Pursuit of a Financial Advisor Field Guide* for finding a financial advisor who will work in your best interests. The Field Guide features information on preparing for your search, the questions to ask, evaluating your advisor, and much more.

Consider the fee an investment in yourself, your peace of mind, and your future.

# Financial Action Plan

| YEAR | Monthly Income | Monthly Expenses | Total Savings & assets | Total Debt | Gap | Education Training | Start a Business or a job search |
|------|------|------|------|------|------|------|------|
| 20XX | | | | | | | |
| | | | | | | | |
| | | | | | | | |
| | | | | | | | |
| | | | | | | | |
| | | | | | | | |
| | | | | | | | |
| | | | | | | | |
| | | | | | | | |
| | | | | | | | |
| | | | | | | | |

copyright 2013 Jean Shaffer

## Resources
- **Retirement Planning**
    - www.ssa.gov/estimator
    - www.aarp.org
    - www.choosetosave.org
    - www.janebryantquinn.com
    - www.smartaboutmoney.org

- **Fee based Financial Advisors**
    - www.napfa.org
    - www.garretplanningnetwork.com
    - www.cambridgeadvisors.com

**Ray of Light**– *Recently, I was listening to a guest on a radio talk show discuss reinventing himself in his 70's to teach fitness classes to senior citizens. Many callers called in with their own inspiring stories. It's amazing how many people in their 60's and 70's are teaching fitness classes. Some were pursuing advanced degrees, and others shared stories about their parents well into their 80's and 90's working part-time and full-time with no plan for retirement. We Baby Boomers are awesome! We are going to change the way the world thinks of retirement.*

**One Small Step –**

**Today, I am grateful for –**

# Chapter 5

*They Don't Appreciate Me.*

I am tired of working so hard, and feel angry when I think about how my current or former employers have disappointed me.

If you answered *Agree*, it's time to let go of the past. Today is the day to REALLY let go. The world of work looks very different than it did in the 70's, 80's, 90's, and even since 2008.  Do we really think that we will be dealing with the same reality in 5 years or 10 years? Who knows?  The younger generations are and will be more fun to work with.

*When one door closes*
*Another door opens*
*But we so often look so long*
*And so regretfully*
*Upon the closed door*
*That we do not see the ones*
*Which open for us.*
*– Alexander Graham Bell*

In the field of Training & Development, we must consider knowledge, skills, and attitudes in every learning objective.  All of these have relevance whether we are talking about careers or finance.

I've always liked this quote by Alexander Graham Bell because it reminds me to pay attention to opportunities that are presented to me on a daily basis.

It's important to ask yourself if your view of the past could be preventing you from seeing the future in a new light or from recognizing opportunities in the present moment.

Reframing our attitude about the future starts with having an open mind that allows you to consider and create a new vision for the future.  How would you love to spend your time?

If I asked you to describe in detail what you want your future to look like, could you do it?   What if I asked you to describe what you are afraid of?  Which answer has more detail?  If you have a clear and vivid vision of what you want your life to look like, then you are light years ahead of most of us.

*I can teach anybody how to get what they want out of life. The problem is that I can't find anybody who can tell me what they want. – **Mark Twain***

Frequently, when working with clients on a job search, they are reluctant to tell me what their ideal job would be; however, they are clear about what they don't want to do. Why not figure out what the ideal career would be, and pursue that? Somewhere in that ideal vision is something attainable.

I've noticed that women are more likely to have vision boards. However, I've noticed that successful male motivational speakers are likely to have a clear vision of their future.

Shame on me. Recently, it occurred to me that my vision didn't go beyond my 60s. That was a huge "light bulb moment" for me. So, I created a PowerPoint presentation with a slide for each decade, 60, 70, 80, 90. I used Google to find photos of the things I want in my life. With a quick copy and paste, I had my vision board for each decade. It was fun, inspiring and exhilarating.

I'm also learning to be more grateful for what I already have in my life. It's so easy to overlook the people and things we take for granted.

**Ray of Light** – *Jack, a client of mine in his late 50's, was in a sales position, working from home, no travel, and good income. He was frustrated with management and felt unappreciated. We looked at his values, interests, skills, accomplishments, and goals. We identified a great bridge to retirement job as a Healthcare Advocate. However, because of the recession, he decided to postpone this career change. We discussed how to come to terms with feeling unappreciated, and how to nurture relationships with management. Sometimes, we can find joy in our current position, if we look around the edges. My favorite question to myself is, "How can I make this work for me?"*

**One Small Step** –

**Today, I am grateful for** –

# *Chapter 6*

## *Who's in control of your life?*

Each year I assess my talents and reflect on what I enjoy, and seek out projects that energize me.

*The privilege of a lifetime is being who you are.* – **Joseph Campbell**

If you answered *Agree*, BRAVO. If not, I suggest that you read *Putting Your Strengths to Work* by Marcus Buckingham. Identify your best skills that you enjoy using, and figure out where and how you could use those to make a difference. Who would value your knowledge and experience? Look for opportunities to showcase your talents, volunteer for special/additional projects.

Frequently, clients have said to me, "I don't have any passions," and yet after some discussion I learn that they love history or baseball or cleaning and organizing. So, what is a passion? It can simply be an area of strong interest, something you really enjoy reading or talking about. A passion can also be a really strong value, something you want in your life.

I recognized in my mid-thirties that I needed to have some aspect of creativity in my work life to be happy in my work. I've also recognized that I am happiest when I have creative projects in my work and personal life.

My favorite technique for relaxation is music. I love to listen to Soundscapes when I'm trying to focus or work creatively. It's like magic for me. In a stressful situation, I remind myself to breathe slowly and deeply.

Did you know that while we sleep our brains are problem-solving? Have you ever had a great idea in the shower? Or in the middle of the night, that you had to write down? For some of my friends and family members, relaxation is achieved through some physical activity such as running, sports, cooking, or building things. However, there is another level of creativity that can be tapped into through being still.

Sometimes our self-limiting beliefs prevent us from pursuing a path that can offer tremendous satisfaction.

Finding your passions requires quiet reflection and contemplation.

- What inspires you?
    - *Music*
    - *Meditation*
    - *Visualization*
    - *Art*
    - *Nature*
    - *Gardening*
    - *Building*
    - *Relaxation*
    - *Spirituality*
    - *Stories*
    - *Quotes*
    - *Motivational speakers*

Try to avoid letting images of your elderly parents influence your vision of the future. Dare to design the best chapter of your life.

**Ray of Light** – *Ben retired from a purchasing position with the military, worked as a pastor, completed his Masters of Divinity, landed a position in the prison system as a chaplain, and is pursuing a PhD at age 62. He's never been happier.*

**One Small Step –**

**Today, I am grateful for –**

# Chapter 7
*It's never too late, or what have you done lately?*

Each year I review and develop career management/professional development goals that include networking with other professionals and joining professional organizations.

If you answered *Agree*, APPLAUSE. Never stop learning! Continue to develop expertise in your field and look for opportunities to become the expert in up-and-coming fields, trends, technologies, etc. Expertise can be developed fairly quickly through research, networking, training, and certifications. Advanced degrees should also be considered, but may not be necessary, unless you need the credentials for a new profession or fields such as healthcare or education.

Professional/Career Development goals can focus on any of the following areas:

- Learning – acquiring knowledge and skills

- Networking – learning from others, building relationships
- Professional Organizations – groups in LinkedIn
- Your Brand – developing your reputation
- Industry Trends – following experts in your field or industry in Twitter
- Internal Opportunities – paying attention to organizational shifts and challenges.

I was fortunate to attend a professional development program in my mid 30's, where I realized that career development was my responsibility, not the responsibility of my manager or employer.

Each December, I set goals in all areas of my life, including career development.

Ask yourself:  When was the last time I learned something new?
Am I current on use of smart phones, social media and other emerging technologies?
When was the last time I networked with other professionals?
How many professional organizations do I belong to?
Have I created or updated my Brand?
Am I up to date on trends in my industry?
Am I aware of internal opportunities with my current employer?
What other areas of the organization appeal to me?

Careeronestop.org is a great resource and has information on grants and scholarships available in the US.

☀️**Ray of Light-** *Cathy, a former English teacher, had worked several part-time positions to be available for her school-age child. When she turned 45, she decided to pursue her passion in interior design. She attended a well-known design school, and landed a sales position with a high-end retail furnishings and design firm. After a few years, she launched her own interior design business. She continues to take on new clients at age 70.*

**One Small Step –**

**Today, I am grateful for –**

# *Chapter 8*

*My, how things have changed! And what the heck is branding?*

Each year I update my brand or résumé and spend time researching industry/professional trends and exploring new and challenging topics or opportunities.

If you answered *Agree*, KUDOS. Continue to refine and promote your brand. People must know that you exist. What is your specialty/niche? Social networking is a powerful trend. Professional Associations and networking groups are great vehicles for gaining visibility, growing your network, and keeping abreast of trends and opportunities.

It's so easy to join professional, alumni, and industry groups on LinkedIn.

Twitter gives you access to authors, experts, companies, recruiters, and publications.  Facebook is a great way to keep yourself current and connected with younger generations.  You'll find that you enjoy getting back in touch with old friends, classmates, relatives, and friends of your children.

Two of my friends and colleagues, Debra Fehr Heindel and Danielle Beauparlant Moser, have published a practical and helpful book to help you identify your unique brand.  *FOCUS: Creating Career & Brand Clarity* is available on Amazon.

**Ray of Light**- *A few years ago, I decided to define my professional specialty/niche as "Career Coach specializing in helping Baby Boomers plan to thrive in the next chapters of their careers."  This brand is consistent across LinkedIn, twitter, and my blog.  I volunteer for any project related to my brand, and once a week I share an article through LinkedIn and twitter that is related to my niche.  Last week, I shared an article about a 101 year old man who ran his last marathon.  I received an email from a colleague saying, "you are the queen of Baby Boomer coaches.  Thanks for keeping us inspired."  That made my day.*

**One Small Step –**

**Today, I am grateful for –**

# *Chapter 9*

*If I can just hang in there a few more years.*

I have a transition plan ready to implement, if I lose my job.

If you answered *Disagree*, you may be avoiding the reality of potential job loss. The concept of Portfolio Careers may serve you well during this last phase of your career. If you were forced into early retirement, and if you doubt that you can replace that income or choose to pursue a position with less responsibility or stress, you can consider part-time or contract work as viable options. Also, buying a business or franchise or starting your own business may be excellent options to consider.

Consider or reconsider relocation. Just think about it as a possibility. It could be temporary. Far too many people may be underemployed and over-worked because they limited their search to the local market. Be open to commuting with the option of remote work.

Many Americans have left corporate America for employment in small businesses, government, non-profit, or education. We know that healthcare jobs are seen as the greatest potential for growth. Have you considered any area that would interest you? Have you explored "green" jobs?

Competitors – If moving to a competitor is your plan B, then how prepared are you to do that?

- Knowledge of competitors' products, services, and culture

- Visibility in social networks and groups

- Relationships with hiring managers

- Is your résumé up-to-date?

- Is your LinkedIn profile complete?

Obviously, you have to be mindful of confidentiality, and you don't want your current employer to get wind of your efforts. However, there are things that you can do privately and under the radar, such as research and casual networking conversations. Join professional groups on LinkedIn and start and participate in discussions.

**Ray of Light –** *As a Human Resources Manager, Victor had been through multiple mergers, acquisitions, and reorganizations. HR professionals are in the middle of employee notifications during downsizing, and it is not fun. He was in his late 50's when he decided he had had enough. He relocated to be closer to his grandchildren, and started a business renovating and building new homes. He has been able to ride out the recession and has no regrets. As with many entrepreneurs, his wife returned to work to help with health insurance and provide additional income.*

**One Small Step –**

**Today, I am grateful for –**

# Chapter 10
## *If only I had....*

I sometimes dwell on decisions or choices I made in the past that have had a negative financial impact on me or my family.

If you answered *Disagree*, GREAT. Make the best financial plans and decisions that you can – educate yourself and ask for advice. Question everything and reprioritize your life. How many square feet and bedrooms do you really need? Discuss with your spouse the option of returning to work. Some spouses are returning to the workplace after several years of retirement to supplement the family income or provide health benefits, and while they were initially reluctant, are enjoying the challenge.

Everyone makes mistakes. We can only learn from those mistakes, then let go of the past and focus on what we can do now and in the future. One thing about Baby Boomers is we have been through massive change. We are wiser. We've gained perspective about what's really important.

**Ray of Light** – *My father regretted retiring too early and frequently voiced concerns over his fixed income. However, he developed many interests in retirement, bought a desktop, and wrote his WWII memoirs which was a great legacy to leave to his family. He was able to live a comfortable life. During one of my career transitions, I would catch myself thinking, what if I can't pay my mortgage? I reframed that thought to, what if my next position is the best in my career? Making more money? Working with great people? Try reframing your negative thoughts this way. You'll like it!☺*

**One Small Step** –

**Today, I am grateful for –**

# Chapter 11
*I just want to do my job.*

I stay abreast of trends in my industry and profession.

If you answered *Agree*, CONGRATULATIONS. You have taken a proactive approach to managing your career. If you answered *Disagree*, you could be missing out on the opportunity to establish yourself as a Subject Matter Expert or Thought Leader in your profession or industry. Reading, research, speaking, sharing articles, membership in professional organizations, training, and writing are all strategies for gaining visibility and establishing credibility.

How long does it take to develop expertise on a topic? It's amazing how quickly we can develop expertise through the Internet. We can download books and blogs, articles and research immediately.

In the past, we relied on our employers to pay for all of our professional development. Those resources aren't as readily available as they once were. I have on several occasions invested in certifications that have paid for themselves by making me more qualified for projects.

**Ray of Light** – *Jane had reinvented herself from Flight Attendant, Fraud Investigator, and Copy Editor. She was able to leverage her communications skills, crisis hotline training, and national association experience into a position with a homeless shelter for women and children. She leveraged that experience to land a director position with a small non-profit organization that supports the elderly population. She is still working with the organization at age 66 and considering continuing to work on a part-time basis. Through her volunteer work with her church, she gained experience in strategic planning. She also is considering becoming certified to teach English as a Second Language, maybe in Italy ...who knows?*

**One Small Step** –

**Today, I am grateful for** –

# Chapter 12

*I can help you with that.*

I am aware of opportunities with my current employer and also the challenges and priorities they face in advancing the business.

*Follow your bliss and the universe will open doors for you where there were only walls.* – **Joseph Campbell**

If you answered *Disagree*, you could be missing out on more interesting work, more visibility/recognition, or the opportunity to develop new skills. Listen to your customers, managers, and colleagues when they express needs, challenges, or concerns, and offer to provide a solution. The phrases "I can do that" or "I would like to help you with that," can lead to interesting projects and your professional development.

**☀ Ray of Light** – *After twenty-six years in management, Mark was told his position was being eliminated. He went on a few interviews and recognized that his heart was no longer in this work. After much contemplation and research, he decided to acquire a staffing franchise. Although he was not a sales person, Mark did a great job at sales and networking and cultivating relationships with an "I can help you with that" attitude. He networks consistently through volunteer work with numerous organizations. After a few years, he was able to hire a sales person and his wife handles the business, which frees him to focus on his passion of organizational development and executive coaching.*

**One Small Step** –

**Today, I am grateful for** –

# *Chapter 13*
## *What's age got to do with it?*

So, where do you start – How do you plan for the future?

- Assess the future of your profession and industry
- Identify your values, passions, and talents
- Analyze your financial situation and goals with a Certified Financial Planner
- Research current and future trends of other professions
- Identify and explore options
- Create your vision for the future
- Prioritize your action steps

OK. In 2020, I will be 68. In 2030, I will be 78, and in 2040, I will be 88. My mother is 93. She said, "I never dreamed I would live this long." We need to focus on **what we want** instead of what we don't want. You don't have to know the "how." What energizes you, excites you, interests you, motivates you?

When you reflect back on your life, do you wish you had set smaller goals?  Probably not.  How old will you be in the year 2030?  Whether I like it or not, I will be 78 in the year 2030, I'll be 68 in the year 2020.

I realized that for much of my life, I thought about retirement at age 66, as a time when I will no longer work, and just do what I want to do—hobbies, travel, hang out with friends and family.

However, like many people, I had to realize that retirement is probably not going to happen as I had envisioned it for a number of reasons.

So, it is up to me to create a new vision of my future that makes me feel happy about the future, instead of anxious.  I have been successful in the past at reinventing myself and am now focused on getting excited about the next and best chapters of my life.  I invite you to join me.

*What's Age Got to Do with It?*

We all have watched Hillary reinvent herself from attorney to First Lady to senator to presidential candidate to secretary of state.

I was inspired by Oprah's outlook near the end of the 25th season of OPRAH, as she described feeling like she was just getting started.

Betty White's acting career peaked at age 90. I love to hear her talk about how her life is split between the two things she loves most: animals and acting.

After earning billions, Warren Buffet has expanded his focus to leaving a legacy.

Colonel Sanders opened his first KFC at age 62.

Tony Bennett, 86, continues to record duets with new artists.

Dick Van Dyke, age 87, looking very fit and energetic, accepted the SAG Award for life achievement.

Joan Rivers, 80, hosts the weekly Fashion Police, has a jewelry line which she promotes on a shopping network and is in a reality show with her daughter.

Dorothy Amarandos, 87 year old cellist, who looks 70 and continues to teach.

President Jimmy Carter has advanced through multiple reinventions: US Navy, peanut farmer, state senator, governor, President. He Is considered one of the most successful ex-presidents through involvement with Human Rights, third-world healthcare, Habitat for Humanity, receiving Nobel Peace Prize, and authoring numerous books.

Queen Elizabeth II, didn't even begin to slow down until age 87.

All of these people have the financial resources to kick back and sit in a rocker, but they choose to embrace challenges and lead rewarding lives.

CHANGE INDUSTRIES?

If changing industries is something that interests you, then now is the time to begin your research. Onetonline.org is an excellent resource provided for free by the Department of Labor/Bureau of Labor Statistics. It also provides salary information and projected growth by state for each occupation.

LinkedIn is a great resource for finding contacts by industry.

- Which industries do you find most interesting?

- Which industries would value your expertise, education, and experience?

- Which industries have strong growth forecasts?

- Which industries exist in your local market?

- What are the common threads with your current industry?

- What are the differences with your current industry?

Highlight the common threads and address the differences through research, networking, and training.

CONSULT?

Many of us have functioned as internal consultants and realized that we could offer our expertise to other businesses.  Some people have lucked into lucrative contracts.

A few things to consider:

- Are you prepared for the feast–or–famine nature of consulting?

- Is there a need for your expertise and are people willing to pay for it?

- Do you have consulting skills?

- Are you prepared to do the required marketing/networking?

Once you've been an independent consultant, it's difficult to return to "employee" status. However, many people have tried independent consulting for two to three years and returned to employment as a more predictable option.

An article published in *Consulting Psychology Journal* in 2007 predicts that the leaders of the future will traverse between employment assignments and consulting assignments and will need to maintain their technical knowledge along with the soft skills. They will need to focus on their unique abilities and expertise, not limiting themselves by functions or industries.

CHANGE CAREERS?

Most humans will choose stability over change, and that's why people stay in bad marriages and unsatisfying careers.

Changing careers is an option at any age and deserves exploration.

To make a career change:

- Assess your skills, interests, values, and personality type.

- Determine education or training requirements and expense.

- Network with professionals in the field to gain insights on day to day activities and job requirements. LinkedIn is a great way to find people.

ASSESSING YOUR TALENTS AND INTERESTS AND PERSONALITY

So, where do you start?
You can start with your talents, your passions/interests, or focus on what the experts are predicting for the future.

*DO WHAT YOU ARE* by Paul D. Tieger and Barbara Barron-Tieger is my favorite book to recommend to people looking for the best career fit.

What are professional or industry trends that could create opportunities for you?

Have you considered any of these options for generating additional income?

Additional ideas for encore or retirement careers: Virtual Assistant, Technical Writer, Services for elderly, Esthetician, Wellness Coach, Personal Trainer, Driver, Pastor, Chef, Pet Trainer or Sitter, Tutor, Teach English as a Second Language, Tour Guide, Mediator, Website Developer, Appraiser, Inspector, Home Stager.

Some of the Gen X and Gen Y groups have created their own home-based and lucrative careers by creating blogs and selling to advertisers.

START A BUSINESS?

Many people have dreamed of starting a business. There are so many resources available now to support new business owners, including the Small Business Administration (SBA.gov) and SCORE.org, America's Counselors to small business.

A few things to consider:

- Do you have tolerance for risk?

- Do you have good health, strong drive, and necessary energy required?

- Are you willing to invest time and effort in developing a business plan?

- How much money are you willing to invest?

HELP YOUR SPOUSE FIND A JOB?

**AND The Number 1** favorite career survival strategy is.....drum roll.....help your spouse find a job!! A friend of mine at age 61 cried for 2 weeks when her self-employed husband told her she needed to go back to work for health benefits. She had retired in her early fifties, but found a position as HR Consultant and admits that she's much happier and healthier when she is working. I know other spouses who have done the same thing, working in their spouses' businesses, medical practices or bookkeeping types of positions. Other retirees I know have worked as tour guides and bus drivers for hotels.

- Many spouses are returning to work to provide benefits or supplemental income.

- Former executives are driving tour buses, working as bookkeepers, or internal consultants at lower salaries.

- Selling real estate and teaching will be better options when the economy recovers.

What will your future look like?

When things don't go as planned, we need to get a new plan. Why do we continue to define retirement as a destination instead of a journey? "If I can just hang in there until I'm 66."

How many people have you known who died after they retired, or became alcoholics? I know a few. Why do we think more about what we don't want than what we DO want? If you know the what, you don't have to know the how. Just take a step in the direction of what you want. Don't think you have a passion? Maybe you just haven't discovered it yet. Not everyone has a passion, but most people have values and interests.

CHANGE = OPPORTUNITY

Change does bring all kinds of opportunity, but sometimes we're just not paying attention or drawing on our creative resources to consider how we might tap into future opportunities.

It is exciting to me to hear that our children and grandchildren will be in careers that don't even exist yet.

We are living in an exciting and somewhat frightening time of change that will present all kinds of opportunities. Some of these will involve:

- Technology

- Environment

- Global Economy

- Healthcare

- Aging Population

What opportunities might exist for you in these areas?

BLENDED CAREER PORTFOLIO

When you are talking with a Financial Investment Advisor, you discuss your age, financial goals, family needs and more to determine how much risk would be appropriate in your financial portfolio.

A Blended Career Portfolio approach is an option that allows us to generate multiple streams of income.

This example illustrates how I might use a blended career portfolio strategy to generate income from multiple sources based on my strongest skills and expertise.

# Blended Career Portfolio
## Reduce Your Risk

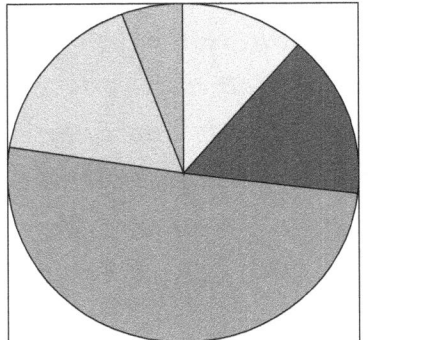

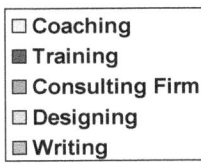
- ☐ Coaching
- ■ Training
- ▨ Consulting Firm
- ☐ Designing
- ▨ Writing

You and you alone have the opportunity to completely redefine your future. Many people have found after retirement that they miss the workplace, the intellectual challenge, and the camaraderie. Not everyone is satisfied gardening, traveling, fishing, golfing, and shopping for twenty-plus years. There are so many exciting options. Why not create the future you want?

And another thing, quit working so hard – try working easy for a change. Ask for help, collaborate, and say "Here's what I CAN do." Do you believe anything is possible? Here's another chance to prove it. Happy planning and see you in the future. It will be here before you know it.

Ray of Light – *Paula Deen tried hanging wallpaper, working as a bank teller, selling real estate and insurance before starting her catering service. She is a cooking show host, author, actress and Emmy Award-winning television personality. She owns and operates The Lady & Sons restaurant in Savannah, Georgia. She has published fourteen cookbooks and has multiple product lines.*

One Small Step –

Today, I am grateful for –

You should now have thirteen small action steps and thirteen things you are grateful for. The only thing we know for sure about the future is that it will change. We are amazing, adaptable, and creative!

So, my friends, next time someone asks how you feel about the future, make sure you tell them...

"My future's so bright, I gotta wear shades."
(Timbuk 3)

## SOURCES

Joseph Campbell, *A Joseph Campbell Companion, Reflections on the Art of Living*, edited by Diane Osbon. Harper Collins Publishers, New York, NY, 1991.

Quotation from *A Joseph Campbell Companion, Reflections on the Art of Living* by Joseph Campbell, 1991, reprinted by permission of the Joseph Campbell Foundation (jcf.org).

Joseph Campbell and The Power of Myth with Bill Moyers. Apostrophe S Productions.

www. AARP.org. *Life Reimagined*.

www.PBS.org. *Age of Champions*.

Mark Twain quote: www.goodreads.com/quotes/69056

Pat McDonald, Timbuk3. *Greetings from Timbuk3*. *"My Future's So Bright, I Gotta wear Shades."* 1986.

## ABOUT THE AUTHOR

Jean Shaffer is a Career Management Consultant with over twenty years experience designing and conducting career and professional development programs. For over thirteen years she has coached tens of thousands of clients in career transition and has been a pioneer in the delivery of career transition services in a virtual environment. She has been affiliated with one of the top global career management firms since 2000.

Jean is passionate about helping mid-life professionals get excited about the next chapters of their careers and future. Her webinar series, *How Bright is My Future?*, provides a practical process that complements pre-retirement planning and provides a roadmap to ensure that people are proactive in assessing their current and future risks, and identifying realistic and inspiring career options.

She holds a BS in Human Resource Development from Georgia State University in Atlanta, GA. She is an MBTI Qualified Assessor and a Certified Job and Career Transition Coach.

Jean works out of her home office in St. Simons Island, Georgia. She can be reached at: jvshaffer@comcast.net, blog: www.jeanshaffer.com, twitter: @jeanshaffer1, www.linkedin.com/in/jeanshaffer.